Cheese! Yummy Cheese!

Start with
a Story

Illustrated by Elisabeth Pulles

Story Idea by Mirna Lawrence
Written by Sue Hepker
workshopped with children from
Orange Grove Primary School

CAMBRIDGE
UNIVERSITY PRESS

It was night time.

The mouse children were having fun in the dairy.

"Let's play hide-and-seek!"

"Who'll be on?" asked Small Mouse.

"Let's choose!" said Tall Mouse.

"Mousy, mousy,
Build a housy.
How many bricks will you use?"
"Fifty!"
"Five, ten, fifteen, twenty, twenty-five, thirty,
thirty-five, forty, forty-five, *fifty*!"

3

"You're on, Big Mouse!" shouted all the mice.
Big Mouse squeezed his eyes shut
and began to count
as all the other mice scurried around
looking for hiding places.
"One... two... three... four... five..."

Small Mouse ran into a corner.
Suddenly she smelled something delicious.
She followed the smell...

5

and nearly bumped into a big red and yellow cheese!
"Cheese! Yummy cheese!" she squeaked excitedly.
All the other mice heard her and rushed to find her.
"Cheese! Yummy cheese!" they cried.

Big Mouse pushed the other mice aside.
"I am the **biggest**!
I should have the cheese!" said Big Mouse.

Then Tall Mouse
pushed in front.
"I am the **tallest**!
I should have the cheese!"
said Tall Mouse.

8

"I am the **widest**!
I should have the cheese!" said Wide Mouse.

"I am the smallest!
I saw it first... " began Small Mouse.

9

But the other mice laughed at her and said,
"You can't have the cheese!"
The mice began pushing and fighting each other.

But someone else had smelled the cheese ...

"Cheese! Yummy cheese!"
said the captain of the army ants.
"Line up!
One ... two!"
All the ants lined up smartly in pairs.

11

The mice were so busy fighting each other
that they didn't notice the ants.
Except for Small Mouse.

She lined up behind the army ants.

"Quick march!"
ordered the captain.
"Left, right, left right,
Lift your knees!
March up for
Your piece of cheese."

"Quick march!"

Two by two, the ants marched
up to the cheese in a straight line.

"One, two,
    One, two,
        A piece for me,
            A piece for you."

14

The cheese got smaller and smaller. When all the ants had taken an equal piece ...

... they marched through a hole in the wall, and disappeared.

Small Mouse quickly took the last piece of cheese.
Meanwhile, Big Mouse had beaten the other mice.
"I win!" said Big Mouse. "I get the cheese!"
But when he turned around, the cheese was gone!
"Mmmmmmmmm," said Small Mouse, with her mouth full.
"Cheese! Yummmmmmmmy cheese!"